CONTENTS

PART 1: ESSENTIAL TIPS BEFORE YOU BEGIN CROCHETING 3

PART 2: REQUIRED MATERIALS 5

PART 3: TERMS AND ABBREVIATIONS 6

PART 4: DETAILED CROCHET INSTRUCTIONS 7

  4.1 SANTA CLAUS 7

    4.1.1 ARM 7

    4.1.2 HEAD 7

    4.1.3 NOSE 8

    4.1.4 MUSTACHES 9

    4.1.5 BEARD 9

    4.1.6 LEG 11

    4.1.7 BODY 12

    4.1.8 GLOVE 14

    4.1.9 HAT 15

  4.2 SNOWMAN 17

    4.2.1 ARM 17

    4.2.2 HEAD 17

    4.2.3 LEG 18

    4.2.4 BODY 19

    4.2.5 HAT 19

    4.2.6 NOSE 21

    4.2.7 HOLLY TREE LEAF 21

4.2.8 LEAF 22

4.2.9 SCARF 22

All rights reserved. This pattern is for personal use only. Please do not copy, resell, share, translate, or distribute any part of this pattern. Crocheters are allowed to make and sell finished products, provided they are not mass-produced, but please credit me as the designer.

PART 1: ESSENTIAL TIPS BEFORE YOU BEGIN CROCHETING

Here are a few important notes to keep in mind before crocheting:

- *Choose the Right Yarn and Hook:* Make sure the yarn and crochet hook sizes are compatible. Check the yarn label for recommended hook size.
- *Practice Basic Stitches:* Familiarize yourself with basic stitches like chain stitch (ch), single crochet (sc), and double crochet (dc), especially if you're a beginner.
- *Check Your Tension:* Keep a consistent tension while crocheting to avoid uneven stitches. You may want to practice a few swatches to find the right tension.
- *Read the Pattern Carefully:* If following a pattern, read through it once before starting. Ensure you understand all abbreviations and instructions.
- *Prepare a Comfortable Workspace:* Make sure you have a well-lit, comfortable area to work in. Take breaks to avoid strain on your hands or wrists.
- *Gauge Matters:* If the pattern provides a gauge, crochet a small test square to ensure your stitches match the required size for the final project.

PART 2: REQUIRED MATERIALS

Name of raw material	Uses
Yarn	There are various types of yarn you can use for crocheting animals, and you can choose any color or thickness you prefer.
Crochet hook	Size 2.5mm or a hook that fits your yarn.
Colored embroidery thread	Embroidery thread adds a beautiful touch to sewing eyes, noses, mouths, and cheeks because its shine gives a more polished look compared to wool.
Yarn needle	This needle is used to weave in the wool and thread after assembling the parts. Wool sewing needles come in various sizes, both large and small.
Polyester fiberfill	Fiberfill suitable is fiberfill balls.
Plastic black safety eyes	Size 8mm
Stitch markers	If you need
Scissors	
Sewing	

PART 3: TERMS AND ABBREVIATIONS

Abbreviations	Definitions
MR	magic ring
ch	chain
sc	single crochet
slst	slip stitch
hdc	half double crochet
hdc-inc	half double crochet increase
inc	increase (two single crochet in one stitch)
dec	decrease (use invisible decrease)
hdc-dec	half double crochet decrease
dc	double crochet
t	treble crochet
BLO	Black loop only
sts	stitch(es)
(…) x n	repeat the instructions in the brackets n times
[n]	total number of stitches in a round
rnd/rnds	round/rounds
M	3 single crochet decrease

PART 4: DETAILED CROCHET INSTRUCTIONS

4.1 SANTA CLAUS

4.1.1 ARM

Start with skin color

Row 1: 6sc in a MR [6]

Row 2: (sc, inc) x 3 [9]

Row 3-5: 9sc [9]

Change to red color

Row 6: 9sc [9]

Row 7: BLO 9sc [9]

Row 8-18: 9sc [9]

Cut the yarn

Attach the white thread for the armholes.

Repeat through ch1, slst row.

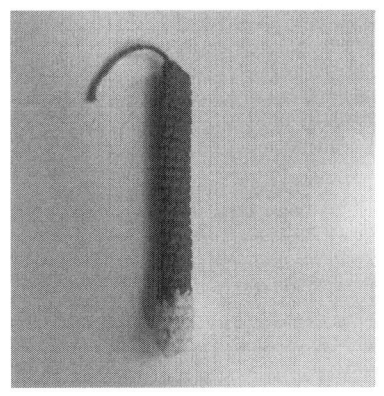

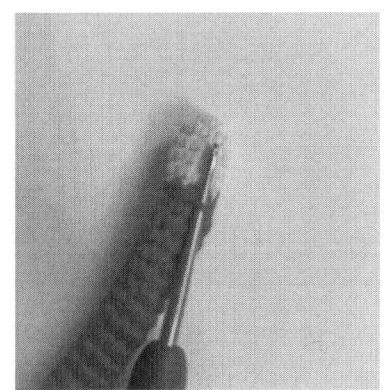

4.1.2 HEAD

Row 1: 6sc in a MR [6]

Row 2: (inc) x 6 [12]

Row 3: (sc, inc) x 6 [18]

Row 4: (inc, 2 sc) x 6 [24]

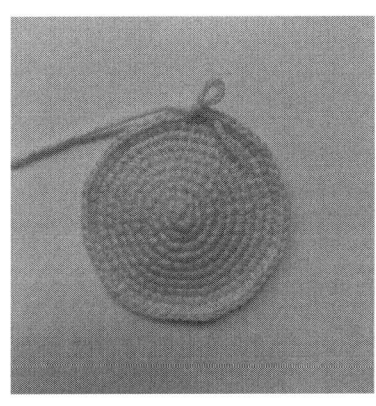

Row 5: (3sc, inc) x 6 [30]

Row 6: 2sc, inc, (4sc, inc) x 5, 2sc [36]

Row 7: (5sc, inc) x 6 [42]

Row 8: 3sc, inc, (6sc, inc) x 5, 3sc [48]

Row 9: (7sc, inc) x 6 [54]

Row 10: 4sc, inc, (8sc, inc) x 5, 4sc [60]

Row 11-24: 60sc [60]

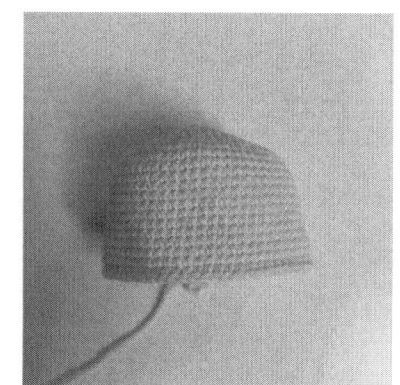

Place the safety eyes between 17th - 18th round. The distance between 2 eyes is 12 stitches.

Row 25: (3sc, dec) x 12 [48]

Row 26: (2sc, dec) x 12 [36]

Row 27: (sc, dec) x 12 [24]

Stuff the head firmly. Cut the color, leave a tail for sewing.

4.1.3 NOSE

Row 1: 6sc in a MR [6]

Row 2: (sc, inc) x 3 [9]

Row 3-4: 9sc [9]

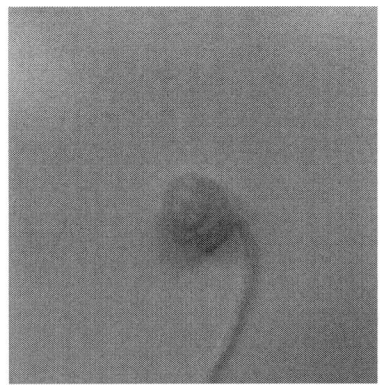

4.1.4 MUSTACHES

Row 1: 6sc in a MR [6]

Row 2: (sc, inc) x 3 [9]

Row 3-4 9sc [9]

Row 5: (sc, dec) x 3 [6]

Row 6: (sc, dec) x 2 [4]

Make two. Leave a tail for sewing

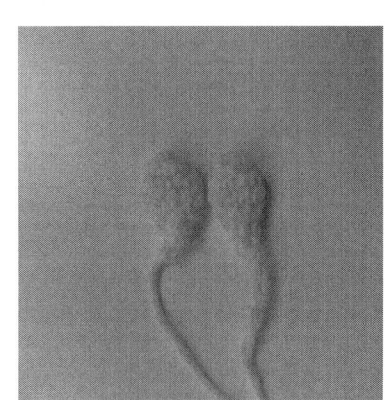

4.1.5 BEARD

<u>BEARD 1</u>

Row 1: ch35, start in second chain from the hook, 34sc [34]

Row 2: (ch5, slst) x 34

Cut the color, leave a tail for sewing

<u>BEARD 2</u>

Row 1: ch33, start in second chain from the hook, 32sc [32]

Row 2: (ch5, slst) x 32

Cut the color, leave a tail for sewing

BEARD 3

Row 1: ch25, start in second chain from the hook, 24sc [24]

Row 2: (ch5, slst) x 24

Cut the color, leave a tail for sewing

BEARD 4

Row 1: ch20, start in second chain from the hook, 19sc [19]

Row 2: (ch5, slst) x 19

Cut the color, leave a tail for sewing

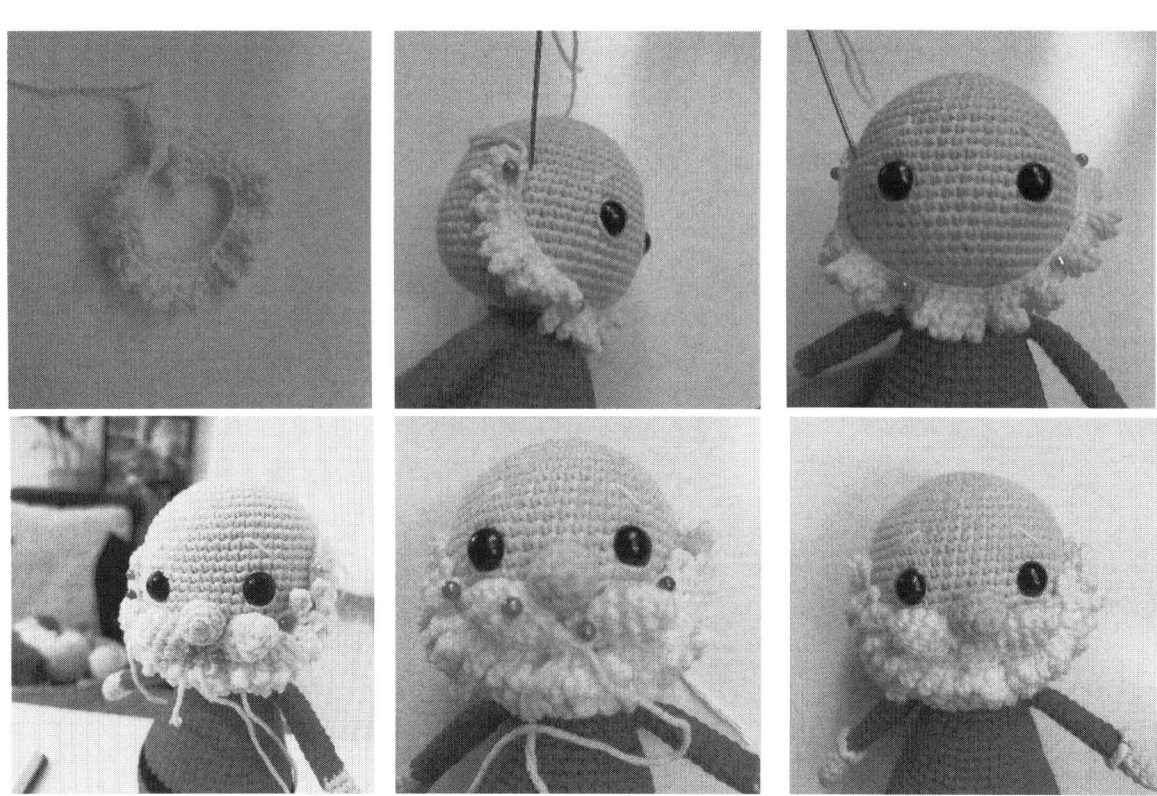

4.1.6 LEG

Start with brown color

ch5, stitches are worked around both sides of the foundation chain.

Row 1: start in second chain from the hook, inc in this stitch, 2sc, 3sc in last st [10]

Row 2: ch1, 2inc, 2sc, 3inc, 2sc, inc, slst in first st [16]

Row 3: ch1, (sc, inc) x 2, 2sc, (sc, inc) x 3, 3sc, inc, slst in first st [22]

Row 4: ch1, BLO sc around, slst in first st [22]

Row 5-6: ch1, sc around [22]

Row 7: ch1, 9sc, 4dec, 5sc, slst in first st [18]

Row 8: ch1, 8sc, 3dec, 4sc, slst in first st [15]

Row 9: FLO ch1, sc around [15]

Attach the red color

Row 10: ch1, BLO sc around [15]

Row 11-13: ch1, sc around [15]

Stuff the leg firmly

Row 14: (2sc, inc) x 5 [20]

Row 15-16: ch1, sc around [20]

Fasten off the first leg. Don't cut the color of the second leg. We are going to connect two legs together.

 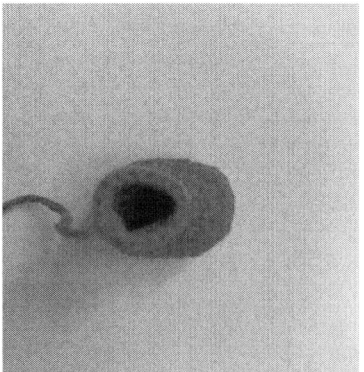 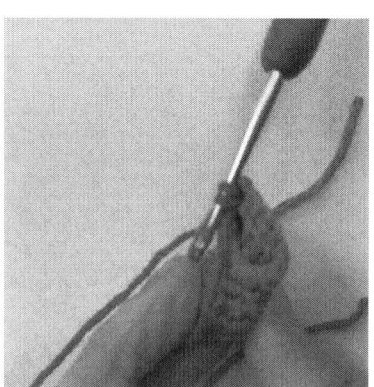
 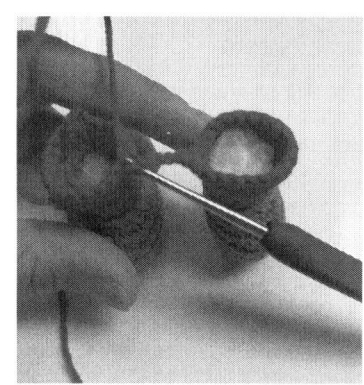 

4.1.7 BODY

ch4, then skip 6 stitches of the first leg (count it from the finished last stitch of round 16), insert your hook in 7th stitch and crochet 20sc around the first leg.

Then make a single crochet it chain stitch and it will be the first stitch of new round and body. Put your stitch marker here.

Row 18: (7sc, inc) x 6 [54]

Row 19-23: 54sc [54]

Row 24: BLO 54sc [54]

Row 25: 54sc [54]

Change to black color

Row 26-28: 54sc [54]

Change to red color

Row 29: (7 sc, dec) x 6 [48]

Row 30-31: 48sc [48]

Row 32: (6 sc, dec) x 6 [42]

Row 33-35: 42sc [42]

Row 36: (5sc, dec) x 6 [36]

Row 37: 36sc [36]

Row 38: (4sc, dec) x 6 [30]

Add arm

Row 39: 10sc body, 3sc body+arm, 12sc body, 3sc body+arm, 2sc body [30]

Row 40: 10sc body, 6sc body+arm, 12sc body, 6sc body+arm, 2sc body [36]

Row 41: (4sc, dec) x 6 [30]

Row 42: (3sc, dec) x 6 [24]

Row 43: 24sc [24]

Attach the red color to the row with BLO.

- (8 sc, inc) x 6 [60]
- 60sc [60]

Change to white color. Repeat through ch1, slst row.

4.1.8 GLOVE

Row 1: 6sc in a MR [6]

Row 2: (sc, inc) x 3 [9]

Row 3: (2sc, inc) x 3 [12]

Row 4-6: 12sc [12]

Row 7: bubble stitch, 11sc [12]

Row 8: (2sc, dec) x 3 [9]

Row 9: 9sc

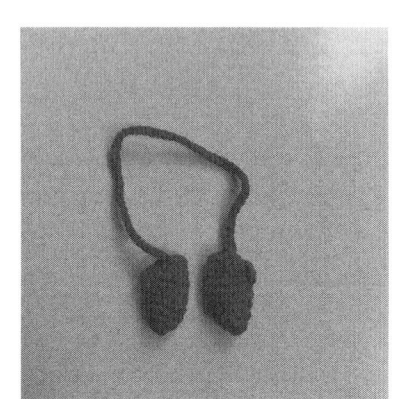

Make two. Join them with 50ch.

4.1.9 HAT

Row 1: 4sc in a MR [4]

Row 2: 4sc [4]

Row 3: (inc) x 4 [8]

Row 4: 8sc [8]

Row 5: (sc, inc) x 4 [12]

Row 6: 12sc [12]

Row 7: (2sc, inc) x 4 [16]

Row 8: 16sc [16]

Row 9: (3sc, inc) x 4 [20]

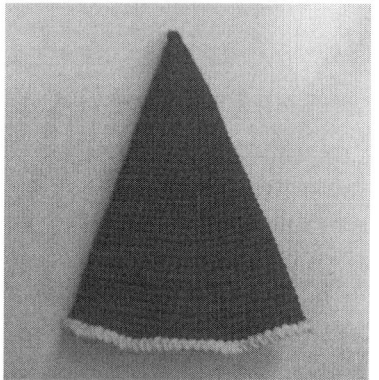

Row 10: 20sc [20]

Row 11: (4sc, inc) x 4 [24]

Row 12-13 24sc [24]

Row 14: (5sc, inc) x 4 [28]

Row 15-16: 28sc [28]

Row 17: (6sc, inc) x 4 [32]

Row 18-19: 32sc [32]

Row 20: (7sc, inc) x 4 [36]

Row 21-22: 36sc [36]

Row 23: (8sc, inc) x 4 [40]

Row 24-25: 40sc [40]

Row 26: (9sc, inc) x 4 [44]

Row 27-28: 44sc [44]

Row 29: (10sc, inc) x 4 [48]

Row 30-31: 48sc [48]

Row 32: (11sc, inc) x 4 [52]

Row 33-34: 52sc [52]

Row 35: (12sc, inc) x 4 [56]

Row 36-37: 56sc [56]

Row 38: (13sc, inc) x 4 [60]

Row 39-40: 60sc [60]

Row 41: (14sc, inc) x 4 [64]

Row 42-43: 64sc [64]

Row 44: (15sc, inc) x 4 [68]

Row 45-46: 68sc [68]

Row 47: (16 sc, inc) x 4 [72]

Row 48-49: 72sc [72]

Cut the yarn, leave a tail for sewing

Repeat across the ch1, slst row with the white color on the last row

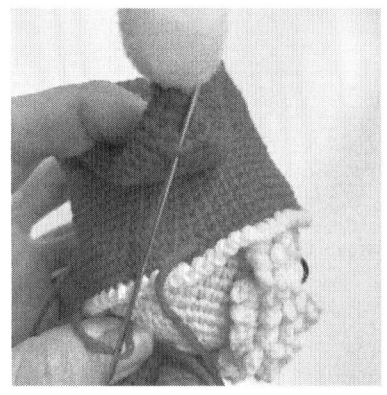

4.2 SNOWMAN

4.2.1 ARM

Row 1: 6sc in a MR [6]

Row 2: (inc) x 6 [12]

Row 3-16: 12sc [12]

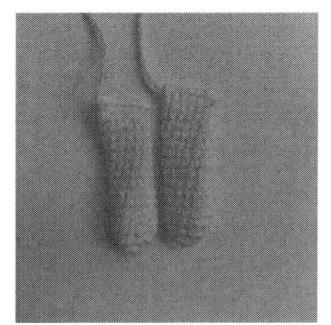

4.2.2 HEAD

Row 1: 6sc in a MR [6]

Row 2: (inc) x 6 [12]

Row 3: (sc, inc) x 6 [18]

Row 4: (inc, 2 sc] x 6 [24]

Row 5: (3sc, inc) x 6 [30]

Row 6: 2sc, inc, (4sc, inc) x 5, 2sc [36]

Row 7: (5sc, inc) x 6 [42]

Row 8: 3sc, inc, (6sc, inc) x 5, 3sc [48]

Row 9: (7 sc, inc) x 6 [54]

Row 10-11: 54sc [54]

Row 12: 4sc, inc, (8 sc, inc) x 5, 4sc [60]

Row 13-14: 60sc [60]

Row 15: (9sc, inc) x 6 [66]

Row 16-18: 66sc [66]

Row 19: 5sc, inc, (10 sc, inc), 5sc [72]

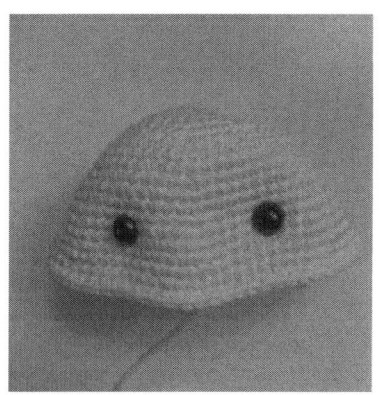

Row 20: 72sc [72]

Place the safety eyes between 16th - 17th round

The distance between 2 eyes is 12 stitches

Row 21: 5sc, dec, (10sc, dec), 5sc [66]

Row 22: (9sc, dec) x 6 [60]

Row 23: (3sc, dec) x 12 [48]

Row 24: (4sc, dec) x 8 [40]

Row 25: (8sc, dec) x 4 [36]

Row 26: 36sc [36]

Row 27: BLO (sc, dec) x 12 [24]

Row 28: (2sc, dec) x 6 [18]

Row 29: (sc, dec) x 6 [12]

Row 30: (dec) x 6 [6]

4.2.3 LEG

Row 1: 6sc in a MR [6]

Row 2: (inc) x 6 [12]

Row 3-4: 12sc [12]

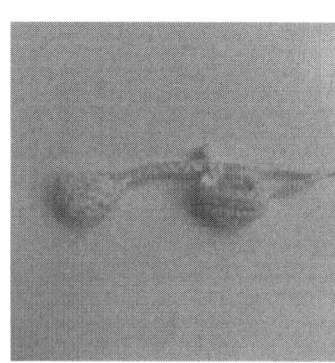
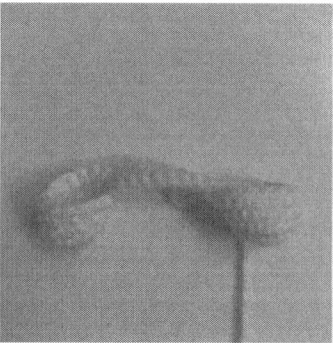

4.2.4 BODY

From the second leg continue crochet 9 chain stitches then connect to the first one.

Row 5: 9ch, leg 12sc, 9sc (on the chain stitches), 12sc leg, 9sc (on the chain stitches) [42]

Row 6-7: 42sc [42]

Row 8: 3sc, inc, (6sc, inc) x 5, 3sc [48]

Row 9: (7sc, inc) x 6 [54]

Row 10: 4sc, inc (8 sc, inc) x 5, 4sc [60]

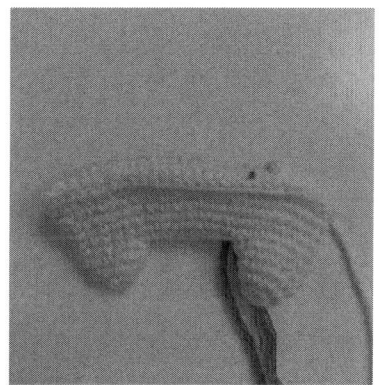

Row 11-20: 60sc [60]

Row 21: 4sc, dec, (8 sc, dec) x 5, 4sc [54]

Row 22-24: 54sc [54]

Row 25: (7sc, dec) x 6 [48]

Row 26-28: 48sc [48]

Row 29: 3sc, dec, (6sc, dec) x 5, 3sc [42]

Row 30: 42sc [42]

Row 31: (5sc, dec) x 6 [36]

Leave a long thread to sew

4.2.5 HAT

Start with brown color or any color you want

Row 1: 8sc in a MR [8]

Row 2: (inc) x 8 [16]

Row 3: (sc, inc) x 8 [24]

Row 4: (inc, 2sc] x 8 [32]

Row 5: (3sc, inc) x 8 [40]

Row 6: 2sc, inc, (4sc, inc) x 7, 2sc [48]

Row 7: (5sc, inc) x 8 [56]

Row 8: 3sc, inc, (6sc, inc) x 7, 3sc [64]

Row 9: BLO 64sc [64]

Row 10-12: 64sc [64]

Row 13: (14sc, dec) x 4 [60]

Row 14-17: 60sc [60]

Change to red color (or any color you want)

Row 18-20: 60sc [60]

Change to brown color (or any color you want)

Row 21: 60sc [60]

Row 22: FLO (4sc, inc) x 12 [72]

Row 23: (5sc, inc) x 12 [84]

Row 24: 3sc, inc, (6sc, inc) x 11, 3sc [96]

Row 25: (7 sc, inc) x 12 [108]

Row 26: 108sc [108]

Cut the rope

4.2.6 NOSE

Row 1: 6sc in a MR [6]

Row 2-3: 6sc [6]

Row 4: (sc, inc) x 3 [9]

Leave a long thread to sew

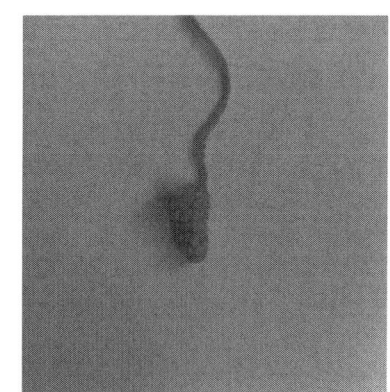

4.2.7 HOLLY TREE LEAF

Start with red color

Row 1: 6sc in a MR [6]

Row 2: (inc) x 6 [12]

Row 3-4: 12sc [12]

Row 5: (dec) x 6 [6]

Leave a long thread to sew

4.2.8 LEAF

Row 1: ch12, starting from 2nd 3sc, ch3, 3sc, ch3, 3sc, ch3, 2sc; cross the chain. 2sc, ch3, 3sc, ch3, 3sc, ch3, 3sc, slst.

Leave a long thread to sew

4.2.9 SCARF

I made 2 sizes

- Green: Row 1: ch112, starting from 2nd 110 dc.
- Red: Row 1: ch82, starting from 2nd 80 dc.

And you're done!

Thank you so much for purchasing my pattern! If you encounter any issues while working with it, feel free to send me a direct message. Thanks again!

Printed in Dunstable, United Kingdom